To Vanessa
With love from G
xx

The Secret of Water

For the Children of the World

Masaru Emoto

SIMON & SCHUSTER

BEYOND WORDS Publishing

Originally published in the English language by
Atria Books   &   Beyond Words Publishing Inc.
1230 Avenue of the Americas   20827 N.W. Cornell Road, Suite 500
New York, N.Y. 10020   Hillsboro, Oregon 97124-9808
USA   USA
www.beyondword.com

This edition first published in the UK in 2006 by
Simon & Schuster UK Ltd.
Africa House
64-78 Kingsway
London WC2B 6AH
A CBS COMPANY

www.simonsays.co.uk

Copyright © 2006 by Beyond Words Publishing Inc.

Photography on pages 16, 18, 19, 21 and 25 provided by Hado Kyoiku-Sha.

This book is copyright under the Berne Convention. No reproduction without permission. All rights reserved. No part of this book may be reproduced or transmitted in any form or by any means, electronic or mechanical, including photocopying or recording, or any information storage and retrieval system, without the prior written permission of Beyond Words Publishing inc., except where permitted by law.

The information contained in this book is intended to be educational. The author and publishers are in no way liable for any use or misuse of the material.

Editors: Michelle McCann and Summer Steele
Managing Editor: Henry Covi
Copy editor/proofreader: Marvin Moore
Cover, interior design and composition: Jerry Soga

1 3 5 7 9 10 8 6 4 2

A CIP catalogue record for this book is available from the British Library

ISBN-13: 978-0-7432-9580-2
ISBN-10: 0-7432-9580-3

Printed in China

The corporate mission of Beyond Words Publishing Inc. – *Inspire to Integrity*

For the children of the world:

Water is very special to me. As a researcher, I have studied it and found that it has many magical qualities. I hope this book will introduce you to the wonders of water so you will grow to love, value, and protect it. As children, you are very special to the world because you are our future. You see things in a bright, hopeful, new way. I hope you hear my message about water and use it to make positive changes for yourself and for our world.

Masaru Emoto

Believe it or not, every thought or feeling you have affects everything around you. Think about it. What happens when you smile at someone? They smile right back! When you share joyful feelings you pass on positive energy and help create joy in other people.

And your feelings don't affect just people. They affect the entire planet. If you speak angry or sad words and think angry or sad thoughts, you will add to the anger and sadness on the earth. But if you speak happy words and think happy thoughts, you will help create a beautiful world.

See how powerful you are? Your feelings affect everything on earth. Even water!

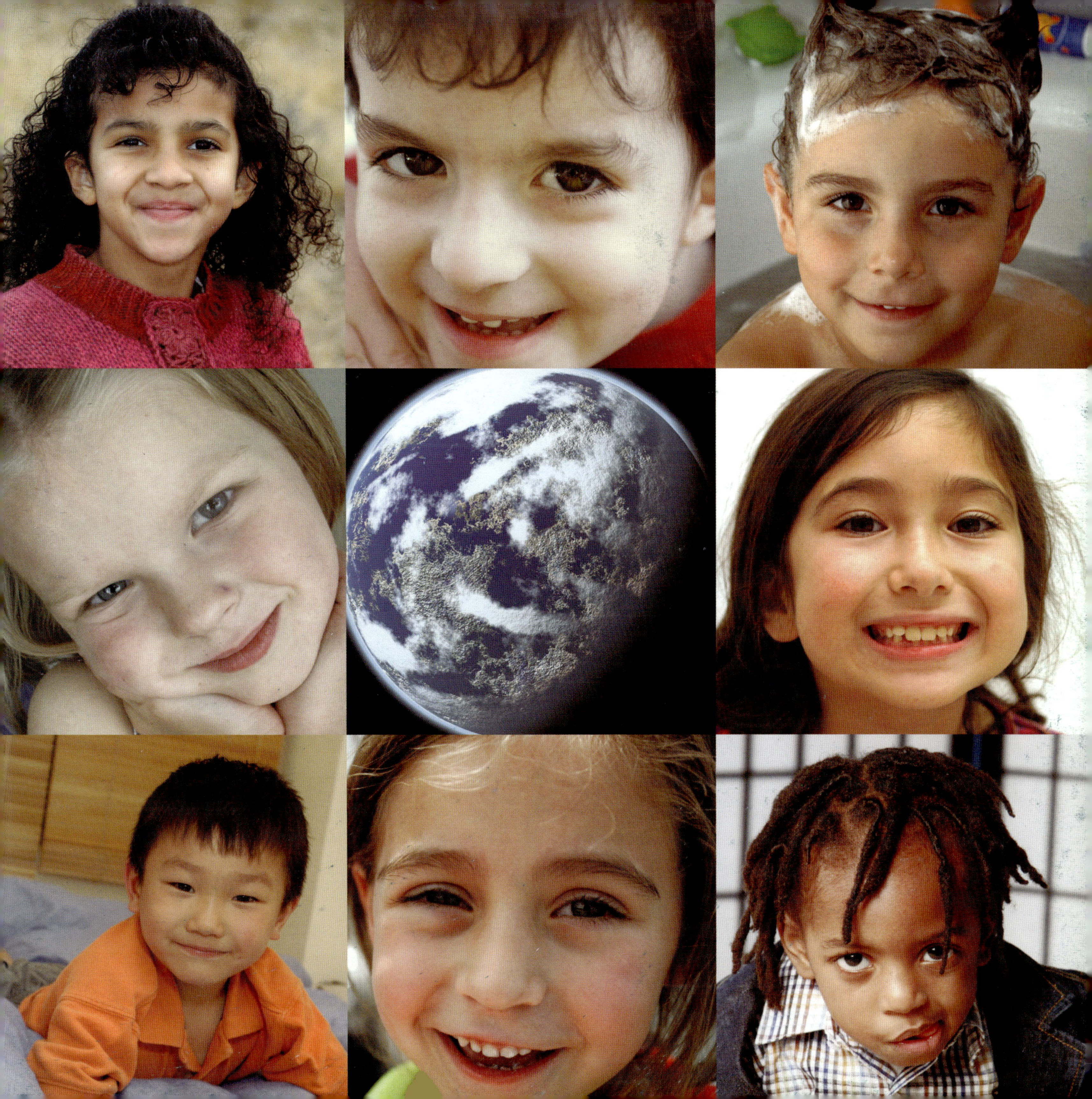

Yes, water. Just as people and all living things are affected by our feelings, so is water. We must do everything we can to make sure water is healthy because it is so important to our lives.

Recently, the United Nations asked all the countries in the world to spend ten years helping water. That means people around the world are thinking of ways to protect water and make it available to everyone.

And guess what? We need your help too!

Let's find out more about water and its secret so you can help.

The United Nations proclaimed the years 2005 to 2015 as the International Water for Life Decade. To learn more about "Water for Life," check out *www.un.org/waterforlifedecade.*

Water has been around a long, long time. It's as old as the dinosaurs! Because of the **cycle of water**, we are still using the same water that once rained down on the dinosaurs millions of years ago. We're drinking the same water the T. rex and triceratops drank! Even raindrops are old. It takes fifty years for a raindrop to fall from the sky and become water on earth.

Most of our planet is covered in water, but we drink just a small amount of it. Much of the earth's water is too salty, too polluted, or too frozen for humans to use. But what we *can* use we *do* use.

What are some of the ways we use water every day?

Water Cycle

Condensation

Precipitation

Evaporation (water vapor)

Collection

Groundwater flow

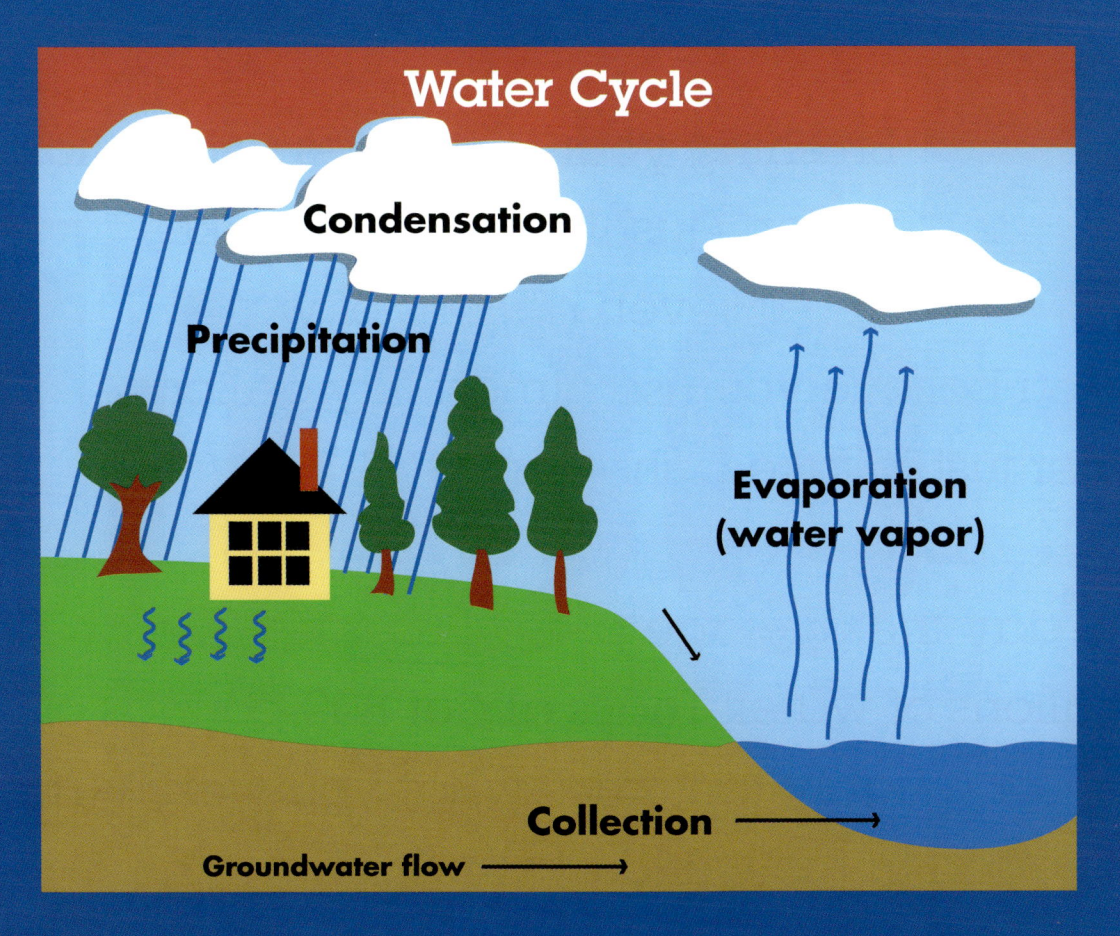

The water cycle has four parts:
1. **Evaporation** is when the sun heats water, turns it into steam (or water vapor), and releases it into the air.
2. **Condensation** is when water vapor in the air cools down and forms clouds.
3. **Precipitation** is when there is so much condensation the clouds can't hold the water anymore, so they drop rain, hail, sleet, or snow.
4. **Collection** is when water falls back to earth. If it falls on land, the water soaks in and joins the groundwater. When it collects in rivers, ponds, lakes, and oceans, the water cycle begins all over again.

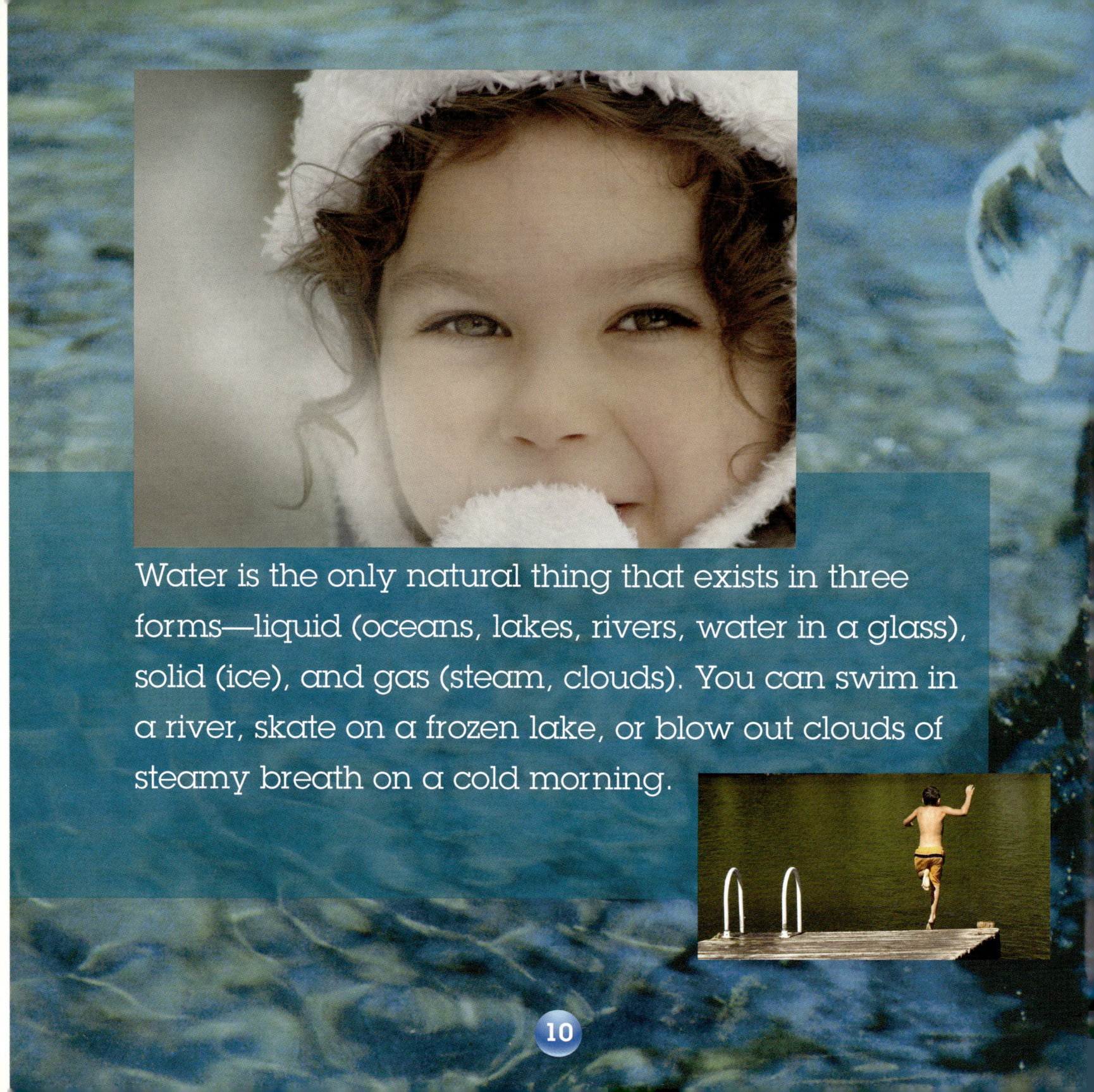

Water is the only natural thing that exists in three forms—liquid (oceans, lakes, rivers, water in a glass), solid (ice), and gas (steam, clouds). You can swim in a river, skate on a frozen lake, or blow out clouds of steamy breath on a cold morning.

Water also has the power to dissolve—or melt—things. It can dissolve almost anything from a lump of sugar to a piece of paper. And water's **surface tension** is so high that many lighter insects are able to walk on it.

Surface tension is the property of water that gives its surface an elastic quality and lets it form into separate drops.

Did you know that most living things are made of water? Your body is filled with bones and muscles and blood, but more than half of what's inside you is water! So much of your body is made of water that you can't live without it. You could live without eating food for more than a month, but your body wouldn't survive a week without drinking water.

Because water makes up so much of our bodies, we have a unique connection to it. The water inside you, me, and everyone else in the world is related to all the rest of the water on earth.

Percent of Water in the Human Body

100% 80% 70% 50%

72%

Our connection to water is what first made me curious about it. I especially wondered about snowflakes, which are made of frozen water. Did you know that each snowflake which falls from the sky makes its own one-of-a-kind crystal pattern? Millions and billions of snowflakes fall to earth every year, and each and every one of them is a completely unique ice crystal. Why?

I began studying water to answer that question and discovered that water responds to good and bad energy through vibration.

Vibration is when something moves or shakes back and forth very quickly. Different vibrations make unique water crystals.

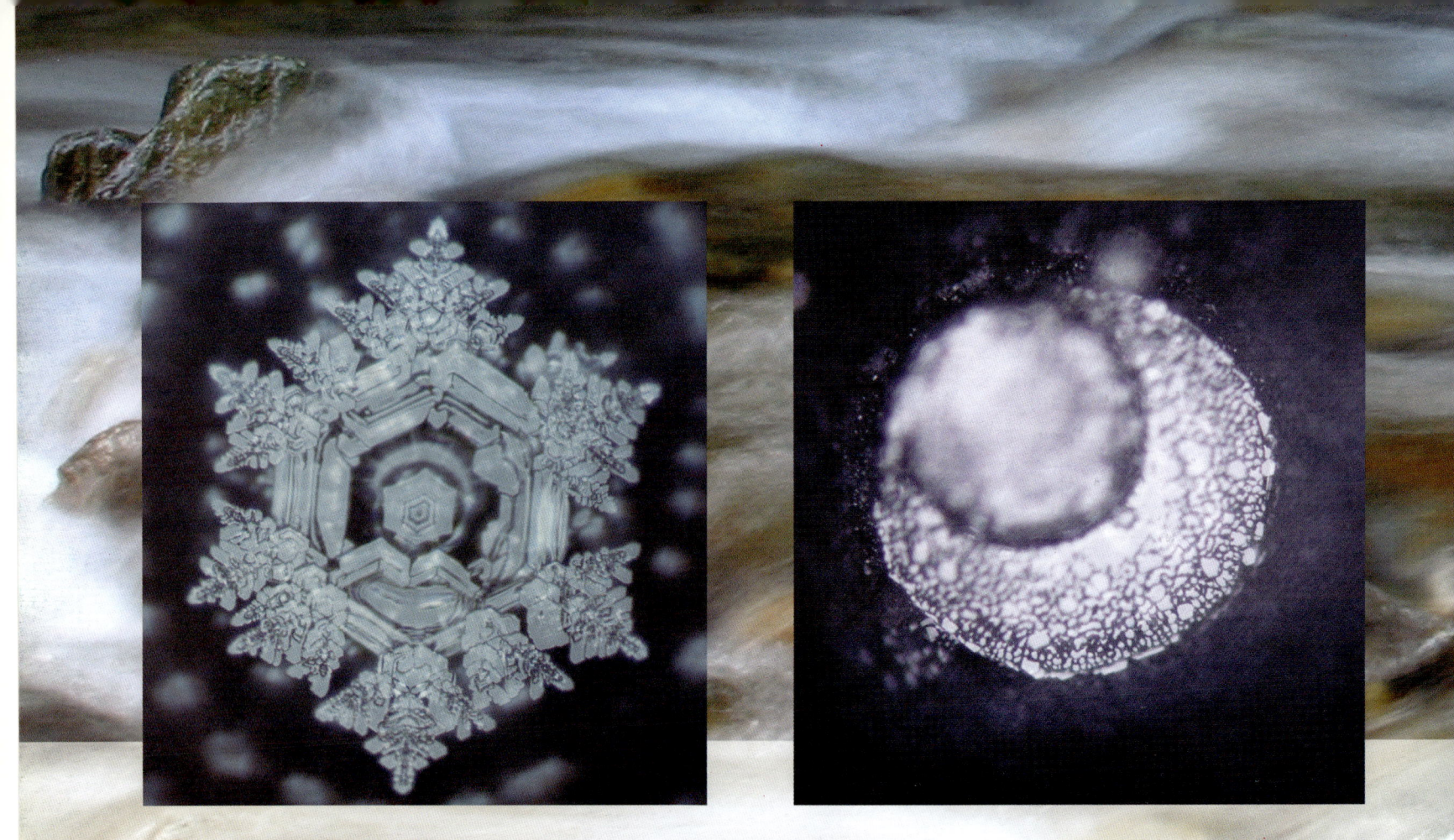

What do you see in these pictures? Some of the pictures are of water that formed crystals when exposed to happy vibrations and other pictures are of water that was exposed to sad vibrations and did not form into crystals.

Can you tell which is which?

This crystal formed after I exposed water to the word "love." The happy energy from that word vibrated the water and made the crystal. Isn't it beautiful?

Here is a photo of water after I exposed it to the words "You fool!" That sent sad energy to the water and it did not create a beautiful crystal.

What do you think a water crystal would look like if you said "thank you" to the water? Let's look at the next page and find out. Can you find "thank you" in your language?

Now you know that we all have the power to affect water. But what can we do with our power? Plenty!

These are crystals that formed after water was exposed to the words "thank you" in each of the languages.

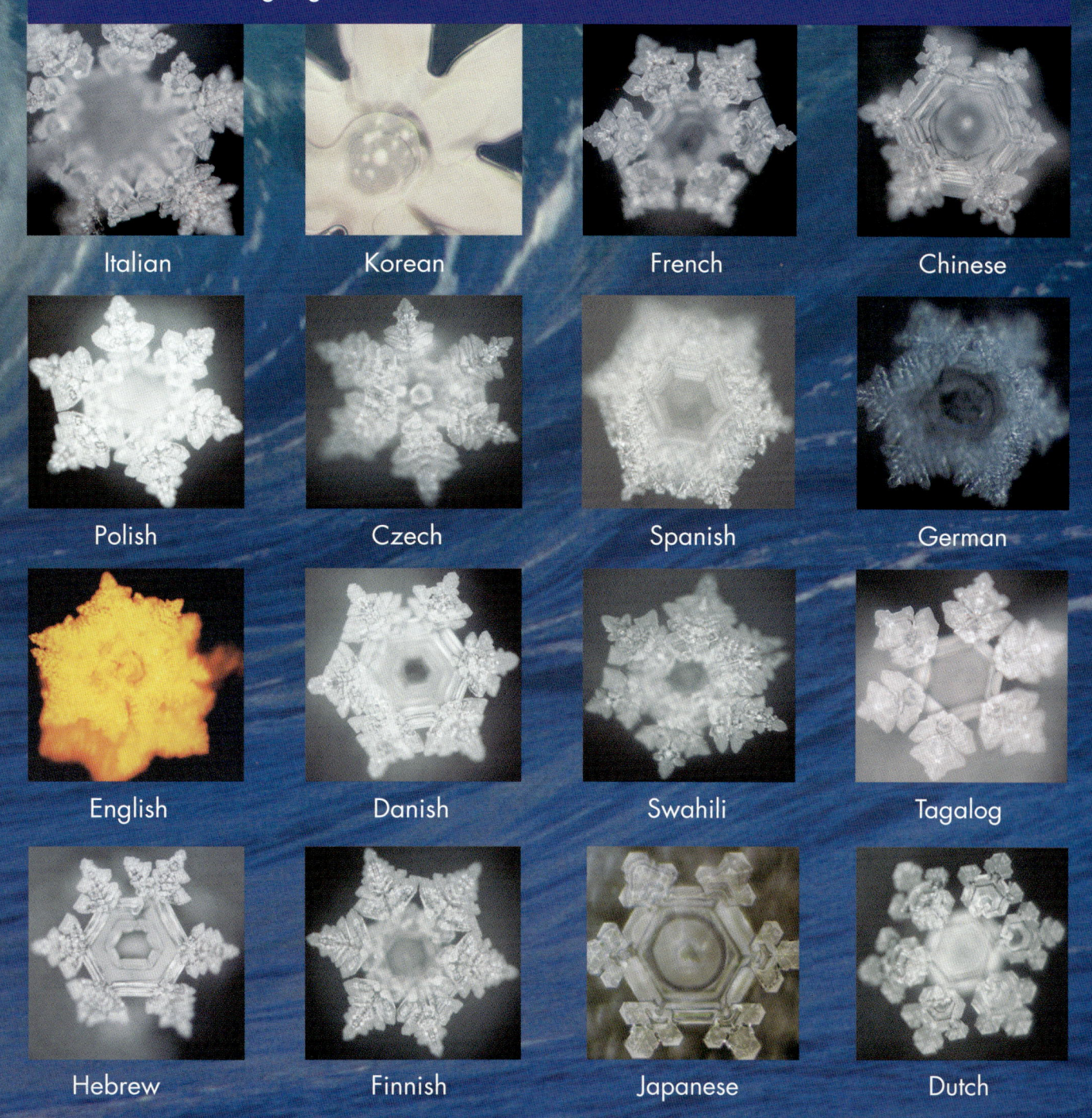

Italian	Korean	French	Chinese
Polish	Czech	Spanish	German
English	Danish	Swahili	Tagalog
Hebrew	Finnish	Japanese	Dutch

21

To help clean and protect the water, we must make water sparkle with love and thanks. When you say or think words of love and thanks to water, your words will dance with water everywhere, and somewhere in the world another person or animal will fill up with your positive energy.

There are many people and animals around the world that need our help. Will you join me and send out your love to those who have suffered through **natural disasters** and **environmental catastrophes**? You can help heal people, animals, land, and water with your happy words and thoughts.

A natural disaster is a destructive event caused by natural forces rather than by human action. Tsunamis, hurricanes, wildfires, floods, droughts, earthquakes, volcanic eruptions, avalanches, and tornadoes can all cause natural disasters.

An environmental catastrophe is a destructive event caused by human activity that damages nature. In 1989 the oil tanker *Exxon Valdez* caused an environmental catastrophe when it spilled millions of gallons of oil into Prince William Sound in Alaska, killing wildlife and damaging the local marine environment.

Water is an amazing gift. It gives us so much—what we need to nourish our bodies, grow our food, and keep ourselves clean. Now it's your turn to give something back to water. Will you help?

Yes, you have the power within you to make water sparkle with happiness and love. Using water, you can heal yourself and others with your happy energy.

That is the secret of water.
Now you know it too. So fill your heart with love and thanks and send your message to all the water in the world!

25

THE SECRET OF WATER IN ACTION

Here are some fun activities you can do to learn more about water and your connection to it.

Clear the Clouds

Can you make clouds disappear using the energy in your mind? You'll never know until you give it a try! To see the clouds better, choose a day with blue skies and white clouds.

What you need: one white cloud

What you do:

1. Relax.
2. Choose one particular cloud in the sky to work with.
3. Focus on that cloud and imagine a beam of light shooting from your forehead into the cloud.
4. While looking at your cloud, imagine it has already disappeared from your sight.
5. While doing step 4, give thanks to the energy that allowed you to make the cloud disappear.
6. Give yourself a few minutes to let your energy do its stuff and then check to see if your cloud is still there. Did it work?

Send Secret Plant Signals

Want to see another way your energy can affect the world around you? Try this game on your own or as a class project for school.

What you need: Two plant seeds (any type of seeds can work, but sunflowers and beans are easy to grow), two cups or containers for planting your seeds, fresh soil, water, two pieces of paper, and a pencil. Ask for a grownup's help if you need it.

What you do:

1. Fill both containers with soil.
2. Use the pencil to poke a small hole into the soil of both containers. Poke your pencil about half way down into the containers.
3. Put one seed in each hole and cover both with soil.
4. Add one teaspoon of water to each container.
5. On one piece of paper write the words "You are beautiful." On another piece of paper write the words "You fool!"
6. Tape the paper with "You are beautiful" to one container and tape "You fool!" to the other.
7. Water the containers once a week and keep them near sunlight.
8. Every time you water the seeds, read aloud the words taped to the containers.
9. Within a few weeks your seedlings should start to grow. Watch for differences between the containers. Is one plant growing faster than the other? Which one looks healthier? What do the results tell you about the power of your words?

Other books by Masaru Emoto

The Hidden Messages in Water

The True Power of Water

The Secret Life of Water

Water Crystal Healing

www.beyondword.com

Resources

Dr. Masaru Emoto

www.masaru-emoto.net

United Nations International Water for Life Decade

www.un.org/waterforlifedecade

The International Water for Life Foundation (IWLF)

www.internationalwaterforlifefoundation.org

IWLF is a not-for-profit organization dedicated to educating and raising the awareness of adults and children about the power of water to affect life on planet earth. Founded in 2006, its mission is to encourage research and collaboration with scientists and organizations to establish protocols and testing of the profound potential of Dr. Emoto's work. IWLF aims to support projects that make clean water accessible to everyone, provide technology for developing water sources for areas in need, and recognize achievements in the arts and sciences related to water.